T0198806

Christmas Caroling
Clearwater Beach, Florida

Erik Raichle graduated from the university with an English Teaching Degree and taught every grade from First Grade thru Twelfth Grade in Pennsylvania, New Jersey, North Dakota, Idaho and Minnesota. He was also a writer for the *Miami Daily* News and thanks Bill Baggs and Damon Runyon Jr. for their help and inspiration.

In 1963, he married Jeanette Motz of Ellendale, Minnesota and together they had nine children and two family bands that traveled all over Minnesota, Iowa and Wisconsin.

For 30 years, he taught in Morristown, Minnesota, where his students sang for governors, produced record albums, published Minnesota's first elementary school newspaper, won the Minnesota state *School Patrol Award*. And, in 1986, his students won the *National Social Studies Olympiad* with the highest score ever recorded. In 1992 and 1998, he was listed in *Who's Who Among America's Teachers* and, in 1989, received the Minnesota Historical Society's *Teacher of Excellence Award*.

To order additional copies of this book, contact:
Xlibris
844-714-8691
www.Xlibris.com
Orders@Xlibris.com

Illustrations by Gil Balbuena Jr.
and Ruth Sanderson

St. Nicholas Church, Tarpon Springs, Florida
Public Domain

ISBN: Softcover   978-1-4797-1008-9
       Hardcover   978-1-4797-1009-6
       EBook   978-1-4797-1010-2

Library of Congress Control Number: 2012916080

Print information available on the last page

Rev. date: 08/03/2021

Yes, There is a Santa Claus!
by Erik Raichle

For as long as I can remember, I've always believed in Santa Claus.

Unfortunately, the last time I asserted my belief so unabashedly, the Third Grade teacher had a "donnybrook" on her hands.

How was I to know, seated in the front row, that I was the only kid in class with my hand raised after she asked the derisive question, "Does anyone in here still believe in Santa Claus?"

As I accompanied her to the principal's office, I felt, not a little, betrayed. If you can't trust your teacher, who can you trust? But, I did learn a lesson from the experience: Keep your beliefs to yourself.

Nevertheless, on crisp December days, as soft snowflakes fall, I get this overwhelming feeling that something great is about to happen. And, I gotta "spread the word", as they say.

This year, however, 'tis different. Unlike other years of my life, I no longer believe in Santa Claus. I no longer believe in him because I know who he is. And, the knowledge is more awesome than the belief.

After years of hiding my bantered belief, I know, beyond the shadow of a doubt, Who Santa is, Where he lives, and Why every living thing on this good earth loves and needs him.

Today, begins a new era in my life.

Scientists and great thinkers of the world, Listen up!

I made my discovery while conducting experiments with photosynthesis.

As I pondered the amazing fact that the flowering green plant can convert the sun's energy into sugar - the requisite nutrient for all life on this earth - my mind took a quantum intuitive leap, and I knew who Santa was.

In my extreme state of exultation, I walked over to the piano and began singing, "Up On The House Top." And, right on cue, the teacher in the classroom directly above mine began stomping vigorously on the floor.

Although the scholarly gentleman had accompanied us many times in the past, on this occasion, he seemed inspired. Perhaps, the May sunshine, streaming through his open window, lighted some poignant memory from a Christmas past.

Now, for the first time, I understood how all those subtle Christmas symbols fit together, like pieces of a giant, joyous, delectable, fruit cake. I understood why Virginia in her famous letter to the *New York Sun* wrote, "If you see it in *The Sun,* it's so." I understood the red poinsettias, the cardinals and holly berries. I understood the green Christmas tree, the Christmas wreath, the mistletoe and all those wonderful songs exhorting us to be jolly. I understood why the first calendars had only 10 months, and how baby New Year, old Father Time and Santa Claus fit into the 10th month, December. And, why the Christmas wreath symbolized the endless circle of time that begins on the 21st day of December. I understood why the first Christmas gifts were good things to eat and the companionship of loved ones.

Ironically, now, that I understand the secret behind Christmas, I can't reveal Santa's identity. After all, if our ancestors, in their joyous design for the holiday, decided to enshroud him in symbol and myth, then I respect their judgment. Certainly, millions of children around the world approve their wisdom. But, I can give you some clues: He's big; he's round; he's red, and he makes you feel good all over. And, without Santa Claus, there'd be no life on this earth.

When I first made my discovery, I felt like shouting it from the housetop. But, quiet reflection reveals that Santa Claus will live as long as the earth revolves around the sun. Mortals merely play out the part which fate has predestined. My part was to reaffirm his existence.

Thus, on

December 21

we celebrate

Sun Day

And, we say,

Happy Sun Day

Then, we decorate our home with

 Red and Green

to represent
The Sun and the Green Plant
because we know that

On December 21, the sun returns, bringing joy, hope, warmth, and life to earth.

He awakens Green Plants to change sun light to Sugar and release Oxygen into the air. Scientists call it Photosynthesis. We need it to live.

He's big. He's round. He's red. And, he makes us feel good all over.
And,

without the Sun, there'd be no life on this earth.

The Spirit Of Christmastime
by Erik Raichle

The spirit of Christmastime, we all agree,
Brings music and laughter to our family.
A tree trimmed with tinsel, its boughs all aglow,
Encircled with garland and sparkl-ing snow.

Beneath the dear tree, lies a village so fair,
With houses, toy trains, tiny cars everywhere.
And, laid in a manger, 'neath heavenly star,
A beautiful baby greets kings from afar.

Look! Santa is waving by our window pane,
So round and so happy to see us again.
He walks to our backdoor with jingl-ing sound
And greets all the children who gather around.

Soon tales of his journey enchant the blithe room
Where our Christmas tree shines in holiday bloom.
How he and the reindeer were busy all night
Delivering presents for children's delight.

Then, seating himself in our old rocking chair,
He opens his book and begins with a glare,
"I hope all you children were good, 'cause you see,
No one who's been naughty gets presents from me."

He carefully checks every good and bad mark,
And finished by telling them this wise remark,
"Now, love one another, be each others friend,
You cannot foretell when your life here will end."

Next, nodding to Brian to bring in the toys,
He reads off the names of the good girls and boys,
"Diana, good Brian, Kurt, Linda, Karlene,
Bright Kevin, sweet Helen, Teresa, the queen."

When Santa had given them every good thing,
And listened to carols they joyfully sing,
He picks up his sack, wishes seasons good cheer,
Walks out of our house saying, "See you next year."

Back to their presents, they race, leap, and holler.
Great Scott! The Gremlins have taken our parlor.
Most wrapping dissolve with an aaah, a giggle.
Others are pondered, then given a wiggle.

Sometime, around midnight, the tempests subside.
They roll out their sleepers and snuggle inside.
With eyes, oh, so heavy, they soon fall asleep,
The spirit of Christmastime kissed on each cheek.

Frank Church
Editor of the *New York Sun*
1897

Yes, Virginia, There is a Santa Claus

by Frank Church

We take pleasure in answering thus prominently the communication below, expressing at the same time our great gratification that its faithful author is numbered among the friends of *The Sun*:

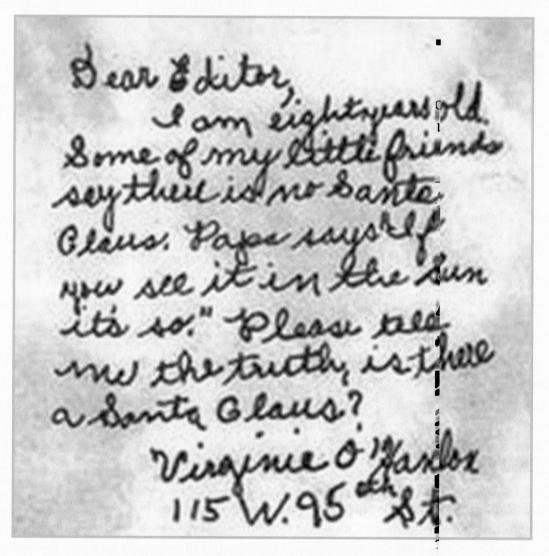

Virginia's letter to the *New York Sun* newspaper

1897

Virginia O'Hanlon

Virginia, your little friends are wrong. They have been affected by the skepticism of a skeptical age. They do not believe except they see. They think that nothing can be which is not comprehensible by their little minds. All minds, Virginia, whether they be men's or children's, are little. In this great universe of ours, man is a mere insect, an ant, in his intellect as compared with the boundless world about him, as measured by the intelligence capable of grasping the whole of truth and knowledge.

Yes, Virginia, there is a Santa Claus. He exists as certainly as love and generosity and devotion exist, and you know that they abound and give to your life its highest beauty and joy. Alas! how dreary would be the world if there were no Santa Claus! It would be as dreary as if there were no Virginias. There would be no childlike faith then, no poetry, no romance to make tolerable this existence. We should have no enjoyment, except in sense and sight. The external light with which childhood fills the world would be extinguished.

Not believe in Santa Claus! You might as well not believe in fairies. You might get your papa to hire men to watch in all the chimneys on Christmas eve to catch Santa Claus, but even if you did not see Santa Claus coming down, what would that prove? Nobody sees Santa Claus, but that is no sign that there is no Santa Claus. The most real things in the world are those that neither children nor men can see. Did you ever see fairies dancing on the lawn? Of course not, but that's no proof that they are not there. Nobody can conceive or imagine all the wonders there are unseen and unseeable in the world.

You tear apart the baby's rattle and see what makes the noise inside, but there is a veil covering the unseen world which, not the strongest man, nor even the united strength of all the strongest men that ever lived, could tear apart. Only faith, poetry, love, romance, can push aside that curtain and view and picture the supernal beauty and glory beyond. Is it all real? Ah, Virginia, in all this world, there is nothing else real and abiding.

No Santa Claus! Thank God! he lives and lives forever. A thousand years from now, Virginia, nay 10 times 10,000 years from now, he will continue to make glad the heart of childhood.

Thomas Nast's famous cartoon of Santa Claus

1881

Henry Livingston, Jr.

1823

The Night Before Christmas

by Henry Livingston, Jr.

Sentinel newspaper

Troy, New York

December 23, 1823

'Twas the night before Christmas, when all through the house
Not a creature was stirring, not even a mouse.
The stockings were hung by the chimney with care
In hopes that St. Nicholas soon would be there.

The children were nestled all snug in their beds,
While visions of sugar-plums danced in their heads.
And mamma in her kerchief, and I in my cap,
Had just settled our brains for a long winter's nap.

When out on the lawn there arose such a clatter,
I sprang from the bed to see what was the matter.
Away to the window I flew like a flash,
Tore open the shutters and threw up the sash.

The moon on the breast of the new-fallen snow
Gave the lustre of mid-day to objects below.
When, what to my wondering eyes should appear,
But a miniature sleigh, and eight tiny reindeer.

With a little old driver, so lively and quick,
I knew in a moment it must be St. Nick.
More rapid than eagles his coursers they came,
And he whistled, and shouted, and called them by name:

Now, **Dasher!** now, **Dancer!** now, **Prancer** and **Vixen!**
On, **Comet!** on, **Cupid!** on, **Donder** and **Blitzen!**
To the top of the porch! to the top of the wall!
Now dash away! dash away! dash away all!"

As dry leaves that before the wild hurricane fly,
When they meet with an obstacle, mount to the sky;
So up to the house-top the coursers they flew,
With the sleigh full of Toys, and St. Nicholas too.

And then, in a twinkling, I heard on the roof
The prancing and pawing of each little hoof.
As I drew in my head, and was turning around,
Down the chimney St. Nicholas came with a bound.

He was dressed all in fur, from his head to his foot,
And his clothes were all tarnished with ashes and soot;
A bundle of Toys he had flung on his back,
And he looked like a peddler just opening his pack.

His eyes—how they twinkled! his dimples how merry!
His cheeks were like roses, his nose like a cherry!
His droll little mouth was drawn up like a bow,
And the beard of his chin was as white as the snow;

The stump of a pipe he held tight in his teeth,
And the smoke it encircled his head like a wreath;
He had a broad face and a little round belly,
That shook when he laughed, like a bowlful of jelly.

He was chubby and plump, a right jolly old elf,
And I laughed when I saw him, in spite of myself;
A wink of his eye and a twist of his head,
Soon gave me to know I had nothing to dread;

He spoke not a word, but went straight to his work,
And filled all the stockings; then turned with a jerk,
And laying his finger aside of his nose,
And giving a nod, up the chimney he rose;

He sprang to his sleigh, to his team gave a whistle,
And away they all flew like the down of a thistle.
But I heard him exclaim, ere he drove out of sight,
"Happy Christmas to all, and to all a good-night."

New Amsterdam

Saint Nicholas and Santa Claus

In the early days of American history, there lived, in the great state of New York, a colony of hard working people, who were called the Dutch.

In fact, the city of New York was not called New York in those days. It was called New Amsterdam, in honor of the Dutch people's home town in Holland.

But, the city changed its name to New York after the English parked a fleet of gun boats in New Amsterdam harbor and told the Dutch to surrender or they'd blow them off the face of the earth.

Now, the Dutch were fearless, but they weren't stupid. And, they had a fearless, crotchety, old leader, at the time, whose name was **Peter Stuyvesant**. And, the Dutch didn't like him too well because he would say mean things, like, "If any man disagrees with me, I'll make him a foot shorter from the top." That meant, of course, he'd chop off their head.

So, when the English naval commander said, Surrender or die. And, the Dutch fearless leader replied, "Over my dead body", it didn't surprise anyone that the good Dutch citizens of New Amsterdam tied Peter Stuyvesant up and handed him over to the English.

And, that's how New Amsterdam became New York, in honor of the English people's home town back in England.

Peter Stuyvesant

Well, for generations, the hard working Dutch farmers and the English farmers lived side by side in the great state of New York. And, they began to marry among themselves and raise families. In fact, Henry Livingston, who wrote *The Night Before Christmas*, had a Dutch mother.

Now, the Dutch celebrated Christmas, just like the English. And, like the English, in the month of December, they had a man, dressed in red, go around town to give presents to good boys and girls.

Only the Dutch didn't call him Father Christmas, they called him Sinter Klass, or Saint Nicholas. And, when the Dutch said, Sinter Klaas, with just the right accent in their voice, their English neighbors thought they were saying, Santa Claus.

And, that, dear reader, is how the world got the name, Santa Claus.

And, that's why our last story is about jolly, old Saint Nicholas.

The Story Of Saint Nicholas

Once upon a time, a long time ago, there lived, in the Greek city of Myra, a wealthy family who had a handsome son, named, Nicholas.

Nicholas was a very, very good and a very, very religious boy.

His mother and father, Epiphanius and Johanna, loved their son very much and gave him everything that money could buy.

But, unbeknownst to them, Nicholas gave his money to the poor. He especially, loved sailors and helped them in every way he could.

Sadly, his dear mother and father died in a plague, and the young boy went to live with his uncle, who was the bishop of Patara.

The bishop noticed Nicholas's goodness and made him a priest. And, when his uncle died, Nicholas became the bishop of Patara.

Soon, Bishop Nicholas's fame spread, far and wide because, not only was he good to people, but also, because God gave him the power to perform miracles.

On one occasion, famine struck the city of Myra, and people were dying from starvation. Now, in the port of Myra, sat a ship full of grain, bound for the Emperor. Bishop Nicholas went to the sailors and asked them to give some of their grain to his starving people. The sailors were afraid because the grain was for the Emperor.

But, Nicholas promised them that if they would help his people, their boat would be full of grain when they reached the Emperor.

The sailors gave their grain to help the people of Myra. And, when they reached the Emperor, the ship was full of grain, just as Nicholas promised.

But, the most famous story of Bishop Nicholas is the story of a poor man who had three daughters who needed a dowry to get married. A dowry was money. And, back in those days, women who didn't have a dowry didn't get married. And, poor girls who didn't get married had very bad things happen to them.

Bishop Nicholas heard about the poor man's plight. So, when the oldest girl became old enough to marry, he threw a bag of gold through the old man's window. And, the next morning when everyone awoke, they found the bag of gold, and the girl was able to marry. When the second girl came of age, Bishop Nicholas did the same thing, and she married. But, when the third girl came of age, the old man became suspicious and hid by the window to see who this mysterious benefactor was.

Bishop Nicolas heard about the man's scheme, so, to fool the old man, he dropped the pouch down the chimney. But, the last daughter washed her stockings that night and hung them by the chimney to dry. And, the bag of gold dropped right into her sock. And, when she awoke in the morning, she found a bag of gold in her sock. And, she was able to marry.

After his death, the church recognized Bishop Nicholas's goodness and called him, Saint Nicholas, or SinterKlass, or Santa Claus.

Ο Άγιος Νικόλαος και ο Santa Claus

Κατά τις πρώτες ημέρες της αμερικανικής ιστορίας, ζούσε, στη μεγάλη πολιτεία της Νέας Υόρκης, μια αποικία από ανθρώπους που εργάζονταν σκληρά, οι οποίοι ονομάζονταν Ολλανδοί.

Στην πραγματικότητα,εκείνον τον καιρό η πόλη της Νέας Υόρκης δεν ονομαζόταν Νέα Υόρκη. Ονομαζόταν New Amsterdam, προς τιμήν μιας πόλης στην Ολλανδία, την πατρίδα του ολλανδικού λαού.

Όμως, η πόλη άλλαξε το όνομά της σε Νέα Υόρκη όταν οι Αγγλοι στάθμευσαν ένα στόλο από σκάφη με όπλα στο λιμάνι του Νέου Άμστερνταμ και είπαν στους Ολλανδούς να παραδοθούν ή θα τους εξαφάνιζαν από το πρόσωπο της γης.

Τώρα, οι Ολλανδοί ήταν άφοβοι, αλλά δεν ήταν ηλίθιοι. Και, είχαν έναν άφοβο, ιδιότροπο, ηληκιωμένον ηγέτη, εκείνη την εποχή, το όνομα του οποίου ήταν Peter Stuyvesant. Και, οι Ολλανδοί δεν τον συμπαθούσαν πάρα πολύ, επειδή έλεγε πράγματα ευτελή, όπως, "Αν κάποιος διαφωνεί μαζί μου, εγώ θα τον κάνω ένα πόδι κοντότερο από την κορυφή." Αυτό σήμαινε , φυσικά, ότι θα του έκοβε το κεφάλι.

Έτσι, όταν ο Αγγλος ναυτικός διοικητής είπε, Παραδοθήτε ή θα πεθάνετε . Και, ο ολλανδός άφοβος ηγέτης απάντησε: «Πάνω από το πτώμα μου", δεν εκξέπληξε κανέναν ότι οι καλοί Ολλανδοί πολίτες του New Amsterdam έδεσαν τον Peter Stuyvesant και τον παρέδωσαν στους Άγγλους.
Και, έτσι το Νέο Άμστερνταμ έγινε Νέα Υόρκη, προς τιμήν της πόλης του αγγλικού λαού στην Αγγλία.

Λοιπόν, για πολλές γενιές, οι σκληρά εργαζόμενοι Ολανδοί αγρότες και οι Αγγλοι αγρότες ζούσαν δίπλα-δίπλα στη μεγάλη πολιτεία της Νέας Υόρκης. Και, άρχισαν να παντρεύονται μεταξύ τους και να μεγαλώνουν οικογένειες. Στην πραγματικότητα, ο Henry Livingston, ο οποίος έγραψε τη Νύχτα Πριν από τα Χριστούγεννα, είχε μια Ολλανδή μητέρα.

Τώρα, η Ολλανδοί γιόρταζαν τα Χριστούγεννα, όπως ακριβώς και οι Αγγλοι. Και, όπως οι Αγγλοι, κατά το μήνα Δεκέμβριο, είχαν έναν άνδρα, ντυμένο στα κόκκινα, να πηγαίνει γύρω στην πόλη και να δίνει δώρα στα καλά αγόρια και κορίτσια.

Μόνο που οι Ολλανδοί δεν τον ονόμαζαν Πατέρα των Χριστουγέννων, τον ονόμαζαν Sinter Klass, ή Αγίο Νικολάο. Και, όταν ο Ολλανδός έλεγε, Sinter Klaas, με ακριβώς τη σωστή προφορά στη φωνή του, οι Άγγλοι γείτονες του νόμιζαν ότι έλεγε, Santa Claus.

Και, έτσι, αγαπητέ αναγνώστη, έγινε παγκοσμίως γνωστό το όνομα, Santa Claus. Και, γι 'αυτό η τελευταία ιστορία μας είναι για τον εύθυμο, γέρο Αγιο Νικόλαο.

Η ιστορία του Αγίου Νικολάου

Μια φορά κι έναν καιρό, πριν από πολλά χρόνια, ζούσε εκεί, στην ελληνική πόλη των Μύρων, μια πλούσια οικογένεια που είχε ένα όμορφο γιο, που ονομαζόταν, Νικόλαος.

Ο Νικόλαος ήταν ένα πολύ, πολύ καλό και πολύ, πολύ θρησκευτικό αγόρι.

Η μητέρα και ο πατέρας του, ο Επιφάνιος και η Ιωάννα, αγαπούσαν το γιο τους πάρα πολύ και του έδωσαν όλα τα υλικά αγαθά.

Αλλά, εν αγνοία τους, ο Νικόλαος έδωσε όλα τα χρήματά του στους φτωχούς. Ιδιαιτέρως , αγαπούσε τους ναυτικούς και τους βοηθούσε με κάθε τρόπο που μπορούσε.

Δυστυχώς, η αγαπητοί του γονείς πέθαναν απο μια επιδημία πανούκλας, και ο νεαρός Νικόλαος πήγε να ζήσει με το θείο του, ο οποίος ήταν επίσκοπος της Patara.

Ο επίσκοπος παρατήρησε την καλωσύνη του Νικολάου και τον έκανε ιερέα. Και, όταν πέθανε ο θείος του, ο Νικόλαος έγινε επίσκοπος της Patara.
Σύντομα, η φήμη του Επισκόπου Νικολάου, ξαπλώθηκε παντού, όχι μόνο γιατί ήταν ο ίδιος καλός με τους ανθρώπους, αλλά επίσης, επειδή ο Θεός του έδωσε τη δύναμη να κάνει θαύματα.

Κάποτε, πείνα έπληξε την πόλη των Μύρων, και οι άνθρωποι πέθαιναν από ασιτεία. Τώρα, στο λιμάνι των Μύρων, ήταν ένα πλοίο γεμάτο σιτάρι που προορίζετο για τον αυτοκράτορα. Ο Επισκόπος Νικόλαος πήγε στους ναύτες και τους ζήτησε να δώσουν λίγο σιτάρι για τους ανθρώπους που πέθαιναν από την πείνα. Οι ναύτες δίσταζαν να δώσουν το σιτάρι, επειδή αυτό προοριζόταν για τον αυτοκράτορα.

Αλλά, ο Νικόλαος τους υποσχέθηκε ότι αν θα βοηθήσουν τους ανθρώπους του, το πλοίο τους θα είναι γεμάτο σιτάρι, όταν θα έφθαναν στον αυτοκράτορα.

Οι ναυτικοί έδωσαν το σιτάρι τους για να βοηθήσουν τους ανθρώπους των Μύρων. Και, όταν έφτασαν στον αυτοκράτορα, το πλοίο τους ήταν γεμάτο σιτάρι, όπως ακριβώς είχε υποσχεθεί ο Νικολάος.

Όμως, η πιο φημισμένη ιστορία του Επισκόπου Νικολάου είναι η ιστορία ενός φτωχού ανθρώπου που είχε τρεις κόρες, που χρειαζόταν προίκα για να παντρευτούν. Προίκα ήταν χρήματα. Και, τον καιρό εκείνο, οι γυναίκες που δεν είχαν προίκα, δεν παντρεύονταν. Και, στα φτωχά κορίτσια που δεν παντρεύονταν, συνέβαιναν άσχημα πράγματα.

Ο Επίσκοπος Νικόλαος άκουσε για το φτωχό άνθρωπο, και το πρόβλημά του. Έτσι, όταν το πρώτο κορίτσι έγινε αρκετά μεγάλο για να παντρευτεί, έριξε μια τσάντα με χρυσό μέσα από το παράθυρο στο σπίτι του γέρου. Έτσι, το επόμενο πρωί όταν ξύπνησαν, βρήκαν την τσάντα του χρυσού, και η κοπέλα ήταν σε θέση να παντρευτεί. Όταν η δεύτερη κοπέλα ενηλικιώθηκε, ο Επίσκοπος Νικόλαος έκανε το ίδιο πράγμα, και παντρεύτηκε και αυτή. Αλλά, όταν η τρίτη κοπέλα ενηλικιώθηκε, ο γέρος άρχισε να έχει υποψίες και κρύφτηκε πίσω από το παράθυρο για να δει ποιος ήταν αυτός ο μυστηριώδης ευεργέτης του

Ο Επίσκοπος Νικόλαος έμαθε για το σχέδιο του ανθρώπου, και έτσι, για να ξεγελάσει τον γέρο, έριξε τη σακούλα κάτω από την καμινάδα. Όμως, η τελευταία κόρη έπλυνε τις κάλτσες της εκείνο το βράδυ και τις κρέμασε στην καμινάδα για να στεγνώσουν. Και, ο σάκος με το χρυσό έπεσε μέσα στην κάλτσα της. Και, όταν ξύπνησε το πρωί, βρήκε μια τσάντα με χρυσό στην κάλτσα της, και έτσι ήταν σε θέση να παντρευτεί. Έτσι λοιπόν, ξεκίνησε και η παράδοση να κρεμάμε τις Χριστουγεννιάτικες κάλτσες στο τζάκι.

Μετά το θάνατό του, η εκκλησία αναγνώρισε την καλωσύνη του Επισκόπου Νικολάου, και τον ονόμασε Αγιο Νικόλαο, ή SinterKlass, ή Santa Claus.

And, now we know that Santa Claus is Greek.
Και, τώρα ξέρουμε ότι ο Άγιος Βασίλης είναι ελληνική.

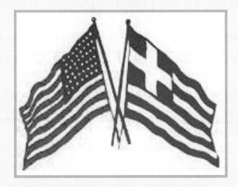

Καλά Χριστούγεννα

Printed in the United States
by Baker & Taylor Publisher Services